# Collision Course!

## Cosmic Impacts and Life on Earth

### FRED BORTZ

THE MILLBROOK PRESS    BROOKFIELD  CONNECTICUT

In memory of Eugene Shoemaker
and in appreciation of Carolyn Shoemaker,
a wise and gentle couple
who, in a single meeting,
had a cosmic impact
on my life as a writer.

Cover photograph courtesy of © J. Baum/Photo Researchers, Inc.
Photographs courtesy of NASA: pp. 4-5 (Donald E. Davis), 8 (D. Padgett/IPAC/Caltech;
W. Brandner/IPAC; K. Stapelfeldt/JPL), 17, 20, 22-23 (Donald E. Davis), 36-37, 42, 52, 61;
James V. Scotti: p. 11; David A. Hardy: pp. 14-15, 58-59; Dr. Alessandro Montanari,
Osservatorio Geologico di Coldigloco, Apiro, Italy: pp. 19, 25, 26; Lawrence Berkeley
National Laboratory: p. 31; Sovfoto/Eastfoto: p. 47; The Minister of Public Works and
Government Services Canada, 2000/Geological Survey of Canada: p. 35; Alan Levenson:
p. 39; Drs. Eugene and Carolyn Shoemaker, David Levy, Palomar Observatory: p. 40

Library of Congress Cataloging-in-Publication Data
Bortz, Alfred B.
Collision course! : cosmic impacts and life on earth / Fred Bortz
p.   cm.
Includes bibliographical references and index
ISBN 0-7613-1403-2 (lib. bdg.)
1. Asteroids—Collisions with Earth—Juvenile literature. 2. Comets—Collisions with Earth—
Juvenile literature. [1. Asteroids.  2. Comets.  3. Disasters.]  I. Title.
QB377.B67    2001
523.44—dc21    00-042706

Published by The Millbrook Press
2 Old New Milford Road
Brookfield, CT 06804
www.millbrookpress.com

# Contents

PROLOGUE    Target Earth!  4

CHAPTER 1    A Distant Rumble: The Solar System Begins  8

CHAPTER 2    Cosmic Weather Report: A Rain of Rocks
and Snowballs  14

CHAPTER 3    Iridium and the Cretaceous Catastrophe  22

CHAPTER 4    The Colossal Crash of Comet
Shoemaker-Levy 9  36

CHAPTER 5    Ogdy's Fireball: The Tunguska Event of 1908  44

CHAPTER 6    Will We See It Coming?  50

CHAPTER 7    Saving the Planet  58

Author's Note  65
For Further Information  68
Index  70

# Target Earth!

**MARCH 13, 1998** did not live up to what superstitious people expected. Instead of being filled with misfortune, that Friday the thirteenth turned out to be Earth's lucky day!

The previous day, newspapers had warned of a possible global calamity. First calculations of the orbit of the newly discovered mile-wide Asteroid 1997 $XF_{11}$ indicated it would come very close to our planet in 2028. It might even be on a collision course! Could the newly released science-fiction movies *Armageddon* and *Deep Impact* be coming true?

Calculating the orbit of an asteroid or comet is difficult, especially when astronomers have no more than a few observations only weeks apart. So they quickly looked for old photographs that might have unnoticed images of the asteroid. Such images—if they existed—would lead to better calculations of the space rock's orbit.

**Regularly** over the history of Earth, big rocks, some the size of mountains, fall from the sky, often changing life on the planet forever.

Luck was with the astronomers—and the rest of us. They found the photographs, and the news from the new calculations was good. Instead of a cosmic close shave at about 50,000 kilometers (30,000 miles)—only one eighth of the distance to the Moon—Asteroid 1997 XF$_{11}$ will miss our planet at a scary but comfortable distance of about 950,000 kilometers (600,000 miles) in 2028. Earth has had many closer calls than that.

In 1908, in the isolated Tunguska region of Siberia in Russia, a giant blast devastated an area half the size of the state of Rhode Island. It was most likely caused by a small comet or asteroid that plowed through Earth's atmosphere, nearly reaching the ground before it exploded.

In 1978 scientists found a surprisingly large amount of the metal called iridium in a layer of 65-million-year-old clay, sandwiched between two layers of rock. The iridium was the first evidence that a 10-kilometer (6-mile)-wide asteroid or comet had hit Earth, setting off a series of environmental calamities that wiped out the dinosaurs and many other species at the end of the Cretaceous Period.

In 1994 telescopes all around the world were focused on Jupiter as more than 20 pieces of Comet Shoemaker-Levy 9 plunged, one after the other for one week, into the planet's cloud tops, leaving dark scars that were visible for years.

The asteroid 1997 $XF_{11}$ scare, the Tunguska event, the "iridium anomaly," and the dramatic end of Comet Shoemaker-Levy 9 all remind us that big rocks can—and do—fall from the sky. Throughout the solar system, countless comets and asteroids, thousands of them large enough to change life on our world forever if they hit, follow paths that cross Earth's orbit.

We should not ask *whether* Earth will experience other cosmic collisions, but *when*. Will we see the rock coming? Will we be able to turn it away or reduce the damage? If it hits, will it destroy cities, our civilization, or even our species? Some of the answers to those questions will be found in science or technology, but others will be found in the minds, skills, and courage of the living creatures who call Target Earth their home.

This book tells the stories of past cosmic collisions. It also describes how people are beginning to prepare for the next one. Though that cosmic *Deep Impact* or *Armageddon* is unlikely to happen in your lifetime, you cannot be certain that it won't. The future of life as we know it may be in the hands of your generation.

Will you and others who share your world be ready?

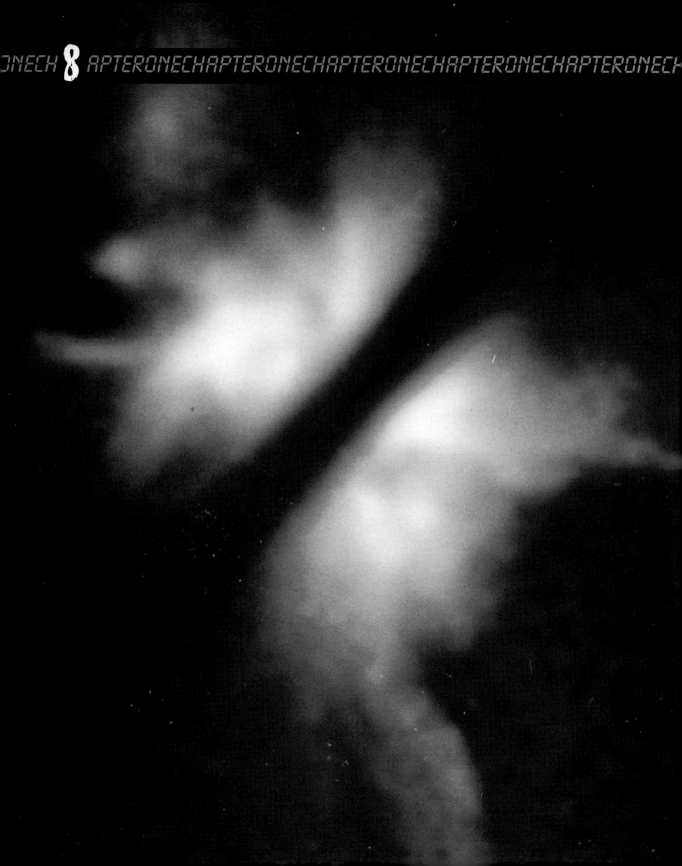

# A Distant Rumble
## The Solar System Begins

*WHERE DO THE ROCKS* that fall from the sky come from? They come from the same matter that formed Earth, the Moon, and the other planets and moons of the solar system.

The story of cosmic collisions begins more than 4.5 billion years ago with a thin cloud of dust and gas slowly drifting and turning in one of the spiral arms of the Milky Way galaxy. Not far away from that cloud in cosmic terms, a star was dying. Like many stars, its end came in a dramatic, sudden explosion. For a short time, the dying star was millions of times brighter than it had ever been.

Had people been around to see it, they would have called it a supernova—from the Latin roots for large (*super*) and new (*nova*). Besides producing a burst of light, the supernova explosion sent the substance of the dying star speeding outward into space. Soon, just as the distant rumble of thunder follows a lightning flash, high-speed debris from the supernova plowed through the peaceful cloud.

**This Hubble Space Telescope** photograph of a newly forming solar nebula shows how the Sun and solar system might have appeared soon after their birth. An edge-on view of a swirling, condensing disk of dust and gas creates a dark streak through the middle of the nebula, hiding the infant star, which illuminates the surrounding thinner cloud of matter.

But this was no ordinary rumble. It was a shock wave, a powerful blast that overwhelms the matter that it passes through. Like a speedboat roaring across a calm lake, it left behind a wake in the once-smooth cloud. Some regions of the cloud now had clumps of matter, while other regions were emptier than before. Quickly the force of gravity began to transform the cloud into a stellar nebula, the dusty birthplace of a star.

The larger the clumps of matter in that nebula, the more powerfully they pulled on other clumps. Soon, most of the matter had been drawn inward to its center. Like an ice skater pulling in her arms, it began to spin faster. The more matter that fell into the nebula's center, the hotter it became. It continued this inward collapse until the central collection of matter became large and hot enough to ignite the process known as nuclear fusion. In that process, matter began transforming itself and producing vast amounts of energy.

The center of the nebula now blazed with light from the star we call the Sun. In orbit around the Sun was the remaining matter of the nebula. Gravity collected small bits of that matter into larger chunks and hunks called planetesimals. Planetesimals collided and then stuck together. The larger they became, the more their gravitational attraction for each other grew.

Soon that process had produced at least ten planets orbiting the Sun, and moons orbiting most of those planets. Countless rocks of varying size also orbited the Sun. Those had escaped being drawn into the newly formed worlds.

**This painting** by James V. Scotti, discoverer of Asteroid 1997 XF$_{11}$, shows the Earth and its newly formed Moon about a year after a collision between Earth and a planet at least as large as Mars. The original cloud of dust and gas, from which the solar system began to form some ten million years earlier, still glows in the sky.

For the moonless, infant Earth and one other planet about the size of Mars, the most powerful impact in their history still lay ahead. Not long after Earth began to cool, the smaller planet smashed into it. That planet was lost forever. Its metal core probably became part of Earth's. Bits of the outer layers of both planets became an orbiting ring of rocky debris around a transformed Earth that was now spinning on a wobbling, tilted axis.

That debris soon collected to form an oversized satellite we call the Moon. The orbiting Moon steadied the wobbling axis like a balance beam steadies a tightrope walker; but the tilt was permanent. Because of that tilt, the pattern of day and night on Earth now varied during its yearly orbit around the Sun. The steady cycle of the seasons had begun.

Many scientists have speculated about what life would be like on Earth had that collision never happened. Besides stabilizing the seasons, the Moon also causes higher tides. Many of today's plant and animal species depend on the tides and the way they wear down rocks into soil.

It is impossible to say what life-forms would have developed on Earth without tides and steady seasons, but we can be certain that things would be very different. Without the Moon, this planet might well have life, but that life would have evolved in very different climates and environments. Without the Moon, human beings—and all the other living species that share our planet today—would not exist in their present form.

We owe our humanity and our position on this planet to a cosmic collision that created the Moon 4.5 billion years ago. As you will discover in the chapters to come, that is not the only cosmic impact that shaped life on Earth!

# Cosmic Weather Report
## A Rain of Rocks and Snowballs

**AFTER** the planets had formed, countless smaller bodies remained in orbit around the Sun. Most of them were bits of dust, tiny rocks, or chunks of ice, but some were large enough to call comets and asteroids. To this day, these pieces—large and small alike—continue to collide with planets, moons, and each other. A cosmic rain of rocks and snowballs continues throughout the solar system.

## British artist David Hardy

recently joined Spaceguard UK, an organization to inform the public of the very real possibility that a large comet or asteroid might strike Earth. This Hardy painting shows a time early in the history of the planet when such collisions were much more frequent as part of a steady rain of cosmic rocks and snowballs.

Day after day, year after year, the planets and moons gain new matter as chunks and hunks, bits and boulders crash into them. Rarely, a planet or moon suffers a great impact from a space rock the size of a mountain. If such a rock did hit Earth, it could upset the balance of the whole planet.

Until the 1980s, few scientists believed that kind of a giant space jolt could happen on Earth. Even fewer had bothered to look for evidence of past impacts. One who did look was famous geologist Eugene ("Gene") Shoemaker (1928–1997). Shoemaker began his scientific career in the early 1950s by diving into the middle of a great scientific argument. Not far from Flagstaff, Arizona, is a circular crater about 1.2 kilometers (4,000 feet) across and about 200 meters (600 feet) deep.

That site is now known informally as Meteor Crater and formally as the Barringer Meteorite Crater after Daniel Barringer. Though leading scientists at the time believed the crater was all that remained of an extinct volcano, Barringer argued forcefully that a huge space rock dug that giant hole in the ground. It was a lonely battle, but Barringer was so certain of his theory that he set up a company to buy the land and mine it for the rich deposit of meteoritic iron and nickel he expected to find.

When Gene Shoemaker began his work at the crater, he and some other scientists already shared Barringer's view. Too many things about the crater seemed peculiar for volcanic activity. A large number of nickel-iron meteorite fragments had been discovered in or near the crater. It was hard to believe that those would have fallen—coincidentally—around an ancient volcano.

The biggest problem with the impact theory was that the meteorite could not be detected. Even the most sensitive instruments could find no sign of it beneath the crater floor. The scientists who supported that theory offered a simple explanation. It was good news for Barringer's theory but not for his mining company. The impact, they said, was so powerful that most of the meteorite vaporized and blew away as dust.

The work of geologist Eugene Shoemaker (1928-1997) demonstrated that the Barringer Meteorite Crater, commonly called Meteor Crater, near Flagstaff, Arizona, was formed by an impact of a nickel-iron space rock about the size of a railroad car less than 50,000 years ago.

So when Shoemaker began his study of the crater, he did not look for the meteorite itself. Instead, he decided to seek signs of its impact in the rocks. It was difficult and painstaking work. He collected rock samples at the crater and analyzed them in the lab. Eventually, a pattern became clear. The usual order of rock layers in the crater was disrupted in a way that could not have been caused by a volcano. Only an impact fit the observations.

Further laboratory work strengthened the theory. Edward Chao, Shoemaker, and Beth Madsen studied bits of shattered quartz from the crater and discovered jumbled crystal structures. This was not ordinary quartz but coesite, a mineral that had previously been found only where the powerful blast of a nuclear weapon had occurred. Even the most powerful volcanoes or earthquakes don't produce enough pressure to turn quartz into coesite. Finally, the scientific world accepted that the crater was created by the impact of a large meteorite.

In addition, coesite and similar minerals now gave scientists a marker to recognize other impact sites, even after their craters were nearly eroded away by wind, rain, flowing water, freezing and thawing ice, plant growth, and animal activity. Because the Meteor Crater is still sharp, it must be young (geologically speaking). Shoemaker's work established that the impact that created it occurred less than 50,000 years ago. For comparison, if we compress all 2 million years of human existence into a day, this impact happened only a half hour ago.

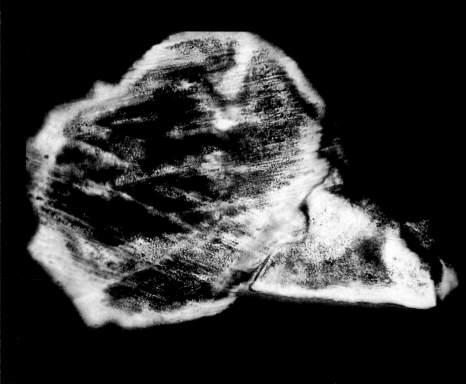

**The work** of Eugene Shoemaker and other scientists demonstrated that powerful impacts caused the disrupted crystal structure of a form of quartz known as coesite, like the grain shown here in a polarized light image. Notice its several distinct crystal directions. This coesite grain formed in the great impact that wiped out the dinosaurs 65 million years ago.

Besides erosion, other natural forces could destroy old craters on Earth or make them hard to find. Earth's crust—the thin upper layer of rock that forms continents, islands, and ocean floor—is not one solid piece. It is made of many moving "plates" that slide over and under each other, creating mountains and erasing landforms on parts of the plates that slide underneath.

Since craters are hard to find on Earth, Shoemaker decided to study the craters of the Moon instead. Without erosion or geological movement to erase craters there, they would last for millions or

**This image** of the heavily cratered South Polar region of the Moon is a composite of about 1,500 photographs from the Clementine mission. Eugene Shoemaker, who read the impact history of both Earth and the Moon in the pattern of craters like these, was particularly interested in the permanently shadowed deep craters near the poles, because they might contain water in the form of ice. Seven grams of Shoemaker's cremated remains, carried aboard the Lunar Prospector, now lie near the lunar south pole, where that spacecraft was deliberately crash-landed at the end of its mission in an attempt to stir up enough ice to be detected.

billions of years. Shoemaker realized he could understand the long history of cosmic impacts on the Moon by carefully studying its pockmarked face. More important, he knew that Earth, with its larger size and more powerful gravity, must have been hit by space rocks even more often than its smaller, less massive satellite.

In the Moon's craters, Shoemaker saw the story of asteroid, comet, and meteorite impacts on our planet. For the first billion years of its history, Earth was pounded by a storm of these impacts. The cosmic fury gradually subsided to a lighter, steady meteoric rain that continues today—but that drizzle has surprises. Once in several million years, we can expect a space rock to smash into

Earth with enough energy to cause serious damage to, or even destroy, the environment of much of the planet.

Soon the National Aeronautics and Space Administration (NASA) began sending spacecraft to and around the Moon. Now Shoemaker and other scientists could study photographs of its previously unseen far side. That turned out to be even more heavily cratered than the near side. When later spacecraft took close-up photos or made radar images of the surfaces of Mars, Venus, and Mercury, they too showed many craters. So did the photographs of some of the moons of the gas-giant outer planets, Jupiter, Saturn, Uranus, and Neptune.

To those scientists, and especially to Gene Shoemaker, the message from all of those images was clear. We on Earth need to be alert for huge rocks that may fall from the sky. We should look for them, catalog them, and track them. We should also think about ways to protect ourselves when we discover a dangerous space rock on a collision course with our planet.

At first, most people thought that was too much fuss from a few images. That thinking changed after a team of researchers from the University of California announced that they had solved one of science's most important puzzles. They had found the cause of the great extinction of dinosaurs and many other plants and animals 65 million years ago at the end of the Mesozoic Era. It was, they declared, an asteroid or comet the size of Mount Everest that fell to Earth—and they had the iridium to prove it!

# Iridium and the Cretaceous Catastrophe

*LIKE GENE SHOEMAKER*, Walter Alvarez loved rocks and the stories they told. As a student at Princeton University in the 1960s, he became part of a team that studied the geology of a peninsula on the northern coast of South America. It was an exciting time because geologists were just beginning to accept that continents moved slowly. His work was one small piece of a great jigsaw puzzle that led to that conclusion.

As the pieces came together, a new picture of the history of life on our planet appeared. The continents, though seemingly solid and unmoving, are in fact drifting slowly over Earth's surface. Oceans and seas, though they appear to be unchanging, slowly open or close, spread or contract. Those changing patterns of land and water seemed to explain the way climate changed and living species evolved throughout our planet's history.

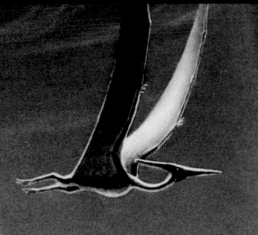

Asaro and Michel's measurements led to the astonishing theory that a space rock as large as a mountain set off a global calamity when it crashed into Earth.

Though everything on Earth changed, the changes seemed to be gradual, slow, and steady—or uniform, to use a word that geologists favored. The theory of plate tectonics was gaining acceptance, and uniformitarianism was firmly established as the guiding scientific principle of geology. Walter Alvarez's research seemed to make that principle even stronger.

Geologists knew that sudden, dramatic events—catastrophes—occurred, but those events didn't seem to matter much in the overall scheme of life. The few geologists who favored catastrophism as an explanation for changes in life on Earth often faced ridicule. Hadn't Charles Darwin's famous work on evolution and natural selection shown that life changed gradually? Now plate tectonics explained one driving force behind those changes.

As is often true, just as scientists settle down with a new theory, a surprising result jolts them out of their comfortable couches. Walter Alvarez, whose early work had strengthened the uniformitarian principle, was about to discover that the catastrophists were right about certain events in Earth's history. In the 1970s he began to take an interest in some unusual limestone called *Scaglia rossa* in the Apennine Mountains near Gubbio, Italy. *Scaglia* describes its scaly or layered structure that made it easy to chip out for use in building. *Rossa* describes its rose-pink color.

Like rock formations around the world, this *Scaglia rossa* recorded the history of Earth in its layers. Before the mountains were thrust upward by a collision of two crustal plates, this limestone had been at the bottom of the sea. Each layer had formed from the shells of sea animals a little more recently than the one below it. It was full of fossils—though not the kind that most people would recognize. These were fossils of *foraminifera*, often referred to as "forams," single-celled life that lived in the ocean, protected by tiny shells. Forams lived in large numbers and provided the food for many larger creatures.

Like all other species on Earth, forams changed over time. Experts could often look at the forams in a layer of limestone and judge the period of Earth's history in which it formed. In the *Scaglia rossa*, it was particularly easy to recognize the time 65 million years ago when the Mesozoic (middle life) Era ended and the Cenozoic (recent life) Era began. In rocks all around the world, the boundary between those eras is abrupt, and the *Scaglia rossa* is no exception.

Underneath the boundary is Mesozoic rock containing fossils of species of plants and animals that suddenly died out. Above the boundary, Cenozoic rock contains fossils of new species that had not existed before. In *Scaglia rossa* limestone, the forams in the highest Mesozoic layer are much larger than the ones in the lowest Cenozoic layer. Between them is a thin layer of clay with no fossils at all. Something happened to cause that dramatic change. Alvarez wanted to know what it was and how long it took. He suspected that clay layer held clues to the answer.

Many people besides scientists like Walter Alvarez take a special interest in that time as well, because

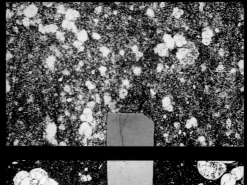

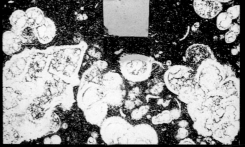

## Though the great extinction at the end of the Cretaceous Period is best known for the end of the dinosaurs, creatures of all kinds died out. This image shows a polished section of Italian limestone containing a thin clay layer placed on top of a pair of microscopic images of the regions above and below that layer. Notice the great difference in size of the tiny sea creatures known as *foraminifera* in the two regions. University of California geology professor Walter Alvarez thought the clay layer might hold the secret of that great extinction.

**Near Gubbio, Italy,** sandwiched between the pink limestone of the Tertiary Period and the white limestone of the Cretaceous is a thin layer of clay about one quarter the size of this 2-centimeter (3/4-inch) coin. Similar clay layers can be found throughout the world.

the Mesozoic Era is better known by the three periods that make it up. The Mesozoic began with the Triassic Period, when large reptiles known as dinosaurs emerged. Next came the Jurassic Period when dinosaurs thrived. The final period was the Cretaceous when dinosaurs may have declined slightly but still ruled the world.

The Cretaceous Period ended suddenly. After 170 million years of Mesozoic life, the dinosaurs were gone, along with about three quarters of all living species. It was followed by the Tertiary Period, the beginning of the Cenozoic Era. In the Cenozoic, with the dinosaurs gone, mammals gradually took over many of the habitats of the world. Eventually human beings emerged.

Geologists call the boundary between Cretaceous and Tertiary rocks the K-T boundary, where *K* is from *kreide*, the German word for "chalk." That describes the form of limestone from that period. They could just as easily use *C* for the Greek root *creta* in Cretaceous, which means the same thing, except that *C* is used for the Cambrian Period when multicelled life first arose on Earth.

In 1977, Walter Alvarez joined the faculty of the University of California at Berkeley, where his father Luis, a Nobel Prize winner in physics for his work with the "zoo" of different particles in cosmic rays, also taught. He brought his father a gift of *Scaglia rossa* that clearly showed the layer of clay at the K-T boundary. They had discussed that rock before, but Luis was busy using cosmic rays to hunt for hidden passages or chambers in the pyramid of Khefren at Giza, Egypt. That project ended with a disappointing result; the pyramid was apparently solid above the known chambers and passageways.

Luis was always on the lookout for an interesting challenge. Now, eager to share an adventure with his son, he turned his attention to another secret hidden in rock. What could they learn from that mysterious layer of apparently ordinary clay in that pink Italian limestone? The first and most important question was how long did it take to deposit the clay.

Walter knew how to use magnetism in the rock as a kind of geologic calendar. His measurements in the limestone showed that the clay layer was deposited in less than 500,000 years, and probably less than 100,000. That was an astonishing result, because such large changes in life-forms normally required millions or tens of millions of years. Could Luis come up with a clever idea to measure that time? The answer was yes, and the secret was to look for the rare metallic element iridium, a member of the platinum family.

Luis knew that iridium and the other platinum metals rain down gently and steadily on Earth as dust from space. That dust is what remains of the countless small space rocks that burn up in the atmosphere. Since Earth formed from planetesimals, it has about the same amount of iridium as the space dust, but with one important difference. The colliding planetesimals created a hot molten ball.

As Earth cooled, heavy nickel-iron sank toward the middle to form the new planet's core, carrying most of the platinum metals with it. The lighter rocks, which hardened to form the crust, had very little iridium. Thus, said Luis, almost all the iridium in the K-T clay layer would be from meteoric dust. He also knew that scientists had measured the yearly meteoric dust-fall. So he and Walter could measure how long the clay took to deposit by measuring the amount of iridium (or another of the platinum metals) in it.

That measurement would not be easy. Though the dust had far more iridium and other platinum metals than Earth's crust did, atoms of those metals were still rare in the dust. Luis calculated that even if the clay layer took 500,000 years to build up, only one atom in 10 billion would be iridium. Ten billion is nearly twice as large as the number of people on Earth. The measurement would be like finding the only iridium ring in the world by checking every person's hands or like finding a needle in a haystack as big as Mount Everest!

Details like that never bothered Luis. He knew that a technique called neutron activation analysis could detect rare atoms by making them glow with particular gamma rays. Since that technique worked best for iridium, that was the metal he chose to look for in the clay. Luis and Walter went to the most careful nuclear chemists they could find, Frank Asaro and Helen Michel, who worked at the university's Lawrence Berkeley Laboratory.

Asaro and Michel had just gotten a new piece of equipment that might barely be able to detect that iridium. They realized that detecting iridium would bring them a lot more work from geologists like Walter. More important, working with Luis would be both fun and a rare opportunity. Although they considered it unlikely that they would detect anything, and they told the Alvarezes so, Luis was not discouraged. He persuaded them that this was a challenge they could not pass up.

It was several months before Asaro and Michel could put a sample of the *Scaglia rossa* clay into their machine. In late June 1978, they finally had an answer. Asaro broke the astonishing news. The measurements showed about a hundred times as much iridium as expected!

The measurements were so surprising that Asaro and Michel were sure at first that something was wrong with their new equipment. They repeated the test, watching carefully for any sign of equipment problems, and got the same results. They had to believe the surprising numbers. What could it possibly mean? Like all good scientists, they came up with one theory after another. Then they did their best to knock those theories down, and they were usually successful.

Finally, Luis suggested something preposterous: The iridium did not come from Earth or the steady fall of meteoric dust. Instead a mountain of rock—a comet or asteroid—had smashed into our planet. Try as they might, they could not find any evidence that went against this crazy idea. Finally, in 1980, they published it in one of the most distinguished scientific journals in the world, *Science* magazine.

Their article triggered a flurry of research that continues to this day. One of the first questions was how that impact—even as large as it was—could have killed off every individual creature of so many species all around the world. Scientists eventually developed this theory: First, the impact raised a worldwide cloud of dust. Huge pieces of rock, blasted high above the atmosphere, fell back to Earth as intensely hot meteorites, setting off forest fires around the world. The dust and smoke blocked sunlight for months, and a global winter set in for many years.

The forest fires produced large amounts of carbon dioxide and water vapor. When the smoke and dust settled, these gases made the atmosphere behave like a greenhouse, allowing solar energy to come through but not letting it out again. The plants and animals that survived the extreme cold soon faced another challenge—extreme heat. Global warming, far beyond anything today's scientists are worried about, quickly set in and lasted for decades or centuries.

**Walter Alvarez** (second from right) gave his father, Nobel Prize-winning physicist Luis Alvarez (right), a rock sample with its curious clay layer as a gift. Luis suggested having a delicate measurement made that might reveal how long it took to deposit the clay. They took the rock to the most careful nuclear chemists they could find, Frank Asaro and Helen Michel.

That wasn't the worst of it. When the comet or asteroid plowed through the atmosphere, it and the air around it became hotter than the Sun. In the extreme heat, oxygen and nitrogen atoms joined to produce nitrogen oxides, which then reacted with water vapor to form nitric acid. The sulfur in the vaporized rocks combined with oxygen and water to produce sulfuric acid.

Soon the planet was bathed in devastating acid rains, corrosive enough to kill plants and dissolve both the shells of water animals and limestone rocks. Besides killing the animals, the dissolving shells and limestone released still more carbon dioxide into the air. Months of worldwide darkness, extreme cold, and acid rain was too much for many plant and small animal species, and they died out completely. The animals that depended on them for food soon followed, and so on up the food chain to the dinosaurs that had managed to survive the cold and fires.

When global warming set in, many of the surviving species also died off. A few—especially smaller animals—were fortunate to find food and shelter. When the climate finally returned to normal, nature was seriously out of balance. That allowed the surviving species to evolve and fill the empty ecological niches. Without dinosaurs—except perhaps small ones that may have been ancestors of today's birds—mammals began to take over the roles once played by reptiles. Over millions of years, large meat-eating mammals—including humans—developed and flourished. Without the Cretaceous catastrophe, our species would not exist.

Once the mass extinction and evolution of new life was understood, a major question still lay ahead. Could we find the impact site, the so-called smoking gun? It wouldn't be easy. Most of Earth is covered by water, so it might be deep beneath the ocean. The shifting of Earth's crust might also have wiped it out. One fifth of the planet's surface from 65 million years ago has been carried beneath other plates and recycled as new rock in the hot interior. If the space mountain hit a continent, 65 million years of erosion would have erased almost every sign of it.

In the 1980s some tantalizing hints began to emerge. At some places in the world, the K-T clay layer had bits of natural glass that came from the melted rock where the impact occurred. As if nature was trying to fool the scientific detectives, these bits resembled the materials of the seafloor. K-T boundary clay from the Rocky Mountains told a different story. It contained quartz with a jumbled crystal structure like the coesite Gene Shoemaker found at Meteor Crater. That suggested the impact was on a continental area, probably in the Americas.

In Texas, geologists studying layers of rock deposited by water found evidence of a giant ancient tsunami—commonly called a tidal wave—around the time of the K-T extinction. Could that have been caused by an impact? If so, it probably hit the ocean. Like the jigsaw puzzle that finally led scientists to understand plate tectonics, it took a while for all the pieces to make sense. Finally it all came together when geologists searching for oil and mineral reserves discovered a huge crater on the edge of the Yucatan Peninsula in Mexico, centered at a town called Chicxulub.

Geologists have since discovered nearly minute-by-minute details of the impact and its consequences in the rocks and seabed. They found bits of soot from forest fires, great jumbles of rock near the impact site, and patterns left behind by a tsunami that sloshed the entire Gulf of Mexico as if an unsteady waiter had carried it in a giant soup bowl. The great story of the K-T boundary is still unfolding as researchers continue to look for more details around the world; but few scientists doubt that a great impact at Chicxulub 65 million years ago suddenly and catastrophically changed the history of life on Earth.

Geologists still believe that uniformitarianism is a great guide to the normal course of change on our planet, but they now accept that an occasional catastrophe can alter that course forever. Those catastrophes are so infrequent that Gene Shoemaker believed he would never see one in his lifetime. Then his wife and colleague Carolyn Shoemaker showed him an odd photographic image of a "squashed" comet. A few months later came the news. That comet was headed for a catastrophic impact with a planet, and no one could do anything to stop it.

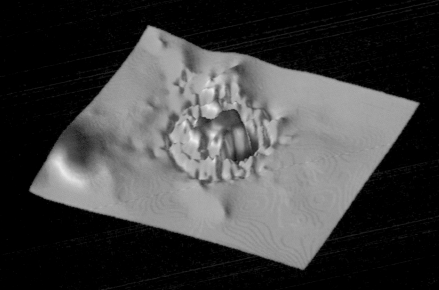

Though the Chicxulub impact crater is not obvious by looking, it shows up clearly in geological measurements. The upper image shows differences in the direction of magnetism in the rocks. The lower image shows small differences in the Earth's gravity.

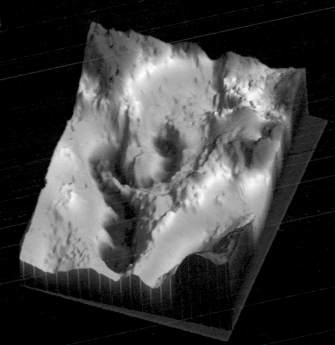

# The Colossal Crash of Comet Shoemaker-Levy 9

**A close-up** of Comet Shoemaker-Levy 9 revealed it to be spread out along its orbit like a brilliant string of pearls. The pieces, designated fragments A through W, were heading for spectacular collisions with Jupiter in July 1994.

*UNLIKE HER HUSBAND*, Gene, Carolyn Shoemaker came to science late in life. In the early 1980s, when Carolyn was just past 50 years old, she asked Gene if he would suggest a project she could work on. It was a question that would change her life.

"I have this little program in searching for asteroids and comets," she recalls him saying, "and maybe you'd like to work in it." Gene had devised a new instrument—a stereomicroscope— that allowed a person to view two photographs of the same part of the sky taken at different times, one with each eye. Anything that moved between the two photos would appear to be floating above the rest of the image. A 45-minute difference between the photos was usually enough to reveal a comet or asteroid that happened to be crossing that region of the sky.

Though the project seemed easy, it required a special person to do it well. Carolyn had all the right traits and abilities. To take photographs through a telescope, she had to pay careful attention to details. She also had to be dedicated to the task. Many times, she would wait hours for a few moments of clear weather on a cold, blustery night.

Once she had the photographs, she would align them carefully in the stereomicroscope. She would scan through hundreds of paired images, most of which revealed nothing new. Her great patience—and sharp eyes—made her ideal for the job. In addition, Carolyn brought the most important quality of all to her work, the insight necessary to recognize a great discovery—if one ever came.

That discovery came for Carolyn Shoemaker on March 25, 1993, after more than a decade of searching the sky. By that time, she had found more comets than any living person. Still, she had never seen a comet that looked like the one in the pair of photographs taken two nights before. She sat up in her chair in astonishment.

"This looks like a squashed comet!" she called out to Gene and their comet-hunting colleague and friend David Levy. Both men took their turns at the eyepieces. Instead of the usual bright nucleus of a comet surrounded by a circular coma and a fuzzy tail streaming outward, this comet appeared to be a bright line of light, pointing roughly east-west, with a bar-shaped coma surrounding it and several tails pointing roughly north. Nearby in the image was the planet Jupiter.

**On March 25, 1993,** renowned comet hunter Carolyn Shoemaker made the discovery of a lifetime at the Mount Palomar Observatory with teammates husband Eugene Shoemaker (right) and David Levy.

They reported their finding by E-mail, and soon observers all over the world were pointing more powerful telescopes toward the neighborhood where the strange comet had first been noticed. The images from those telescopes were even more astounding. Periodic Comet Shoemaker-Levy 9, as it soon would be called, was in fact a chain of comet nuclei, each surrounded by its own coma and each with its own tail. It looked like a string of pearls across the sky.

One discovery followed another. Within two days of its discovery, scientists had enough images of the comet—some unnoticed in photos from as early as March 15—to compute its orbit. They

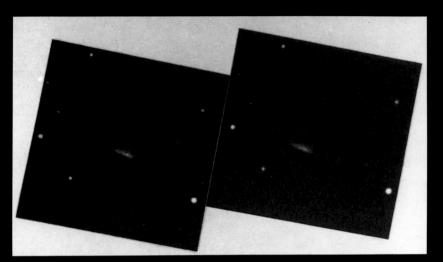

**Good instruments**
and Carolyn Shoemaker's sharp
eyes led to the discovery of
many comets, but these photographic plates were like none
she had ever seen. This comet
was "squashed."

found that it was not merely near Jupiter in the sky, but was actually in orbit around the giant planet. Tracing that orbit backward,
they computed that on July 7, 1992, the comet had come within
20,000 kilometers (13,000 miles) of Jupiter's cloud tops, less than
one third of the planet's radius! At that close approach, Jupiter's
intense gravity pulled the comet to pieces.

Each piece acted like a new comet, shedding fresh dust and ice,
and glowing brightly in the sunlight. To the surprise of many, the
orbital calculations showed that the comet had been orbiting
Jupiter since about 1929, the year Carolyn Shoemaker was born;

but until Jupiter's gravity tore it apart, it was too dim and dark to see. The comet's past was less surprising than its future. This was to be the comet's last orbit. It was on course to collide with Jupiter in mid-July 1994!

The summer of 1994 was one of great anticipation. On Earth, telescopes from backyards to great observatories focused on the collisions to come. In Earth's orbit, the cameras of the Hubble Space Telescope were set to capture images of the great event. The Galileo spacecraft, on its way to a 1996 rendezvous with Jupiter, was also set to send images back to Earth.

Each of the comet's pieces, now designated *A* through *W*, was observed carefully as it approached the planet. The total energy of their impacts was computed to be about the same as the asteroid or comet that struck Earth at the end of the Cretaceous. The pieces were heading toward a point just on the far side of Jupiter, which the planet's rotation would bring into view of Earth within minutes of the impacts.

When fragment *A*—a medium-sized piece—struck Jupiter's atmosphere on July 16, it sent up an unexpectedly bright plume that was visible above the planet's surface almost immediately. Soon afterward, a black spot at the point of impact rotated into view of Earth. This was going to be quite a show! The impacts continued until July 22, but the blemishes in Jupiter's atmosphere—some larger than Earth—could be studied for months.

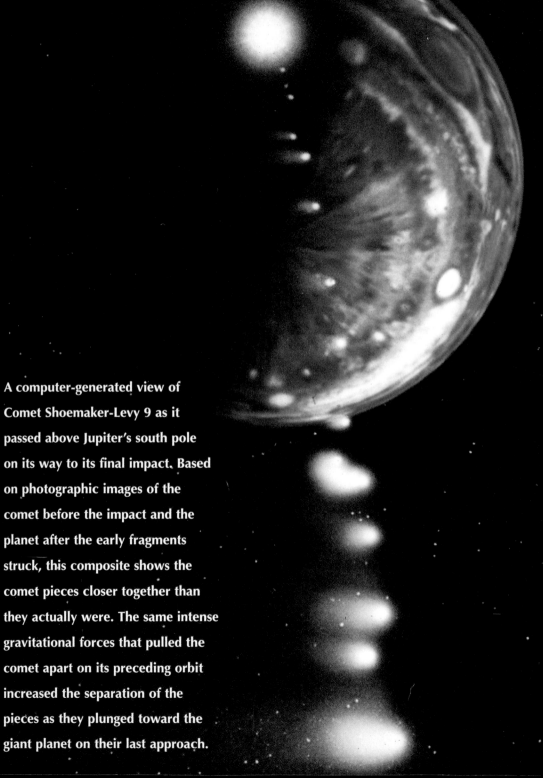

A computer-generated view of Comet Shoemaker-Levy 9 as it passed above Jupiter's south pole on its way to its final impact. Based on photographic images of the comet before the impact and the planet after the early fragments struck, this composite shows the comet pieces closer together than they actually were. The same intense gravitational forces that pulled the comet apart on its preceding orbit increased the separation of the pieces as they plunged toward the giant planet on their last approach.

The colossal crash of Comet Shoemaker-Levy 9 not only taught scientists about Jupiter but also helped them solve a mystery. On Jupiter's largest moons, Ganymede and Callisto, spacecraft had photographed several sets of craters in a row. Most of the sets were on the side of Callisto that always faces Jupiter. Now it was clear: Shoemaker-Levy 9 was not the first comet to be torn apart by Jupiter, and we shouldn't expect it to be the last. This time the comet fragments struck the parent planet and left temporary scars; in the past, other string-of-pearls comets had left permanent marks on those two moons.

Could such an event happen here on Earth? Almost certainly. On the Moon, a line of closely spaced craters crosses an ancient crater known as Davy. Astronomers now believe that a comet or a loosely-held together asteroid brushed Earth's atmosphere and split into fragments that slammed, one after the other, into the Moon. If it happened once, it's bound to happen again. The next great impact on Earth may not come from a single Everest-sized rock like the one that hit Chicxulub. It may be a pounding of 20 rocks, some as large as Pike's Peak, that continues for days.

That would be one for the history books, if anyone is left to write them. If you intend to be one of those future historians, you might want to begin your research with a trip to a remote area in Siberia called Tunguska. The forest there is still scarred from an impact event in 1908, probably the most powerful encounter with an asteroid or comet in recorded history—at least so far!

# Ogdy's Fireball: The Tunguska Event of 1908

DURING late June 1908, peculiar things were happening in the skies above the vast northern region of Russia known as Siberia. Siberia frequently had "white nights" and "noctilucent clouds" in early summer. That year, however, the bright evenings were far more widespread than usual, reaching well into neighboring parts of Europe and middle Asia.

Light from the Sun, never far below the horizon even at midnight in the far northern summer, reflected from high clouds and dust high in the atmosphere. In many European cities, it was bright enough to read the small print of a newspaper or the numbers on a watch face at midnight. During the day, beautiful halos would often surround the Sun. Evenings brought unusual, multicolored twilights. Even if the cause was recognized, no one knew the reason for the unusually large amount of high dust and the unusually large number of high clouds.

On the early morning of June 30, seismographs—instruments to measure earthquakes—detected a tremor in Siberia. That night and the next, the glow in the sky was particularly dramatic, and then the evenings quickly returned to normal. No one connected the two events, not even the scientists at the observatory at Mount Wilson in California, where they noticed that the atmosphere was suddenly less transparent than usual.

The nomadic reindeer-herding Tungus people living near the Podkamennaya (Stony) Tunguska River didn't need a seismograph to tell them what happened. The great fire god of their folklore, Ogdy, was angry, so he sent a fireball brighter than the Sun from the southeast to split the sky apart. The fireball roared like a great battle in the sky. Then, before it vanished in the northwest, it exploded. In the forest beneath the explosion, trees fell outward from the blast, leaving a ring of destruction more than 50 kilometers (30 miles) across. Fire erupted, turning the area into a charred wasteland.

Entire herds of reindeer were wiped out, but by miraculous good fortune, the herders were elsewhere. Only two people are known to have died. Clearly, Ogdy had come to Earth not to kill people, but rather to warn them to change their ways. The zone of destruction was holy ground, and neither Tungus nor outsiders were allowed to enter it for years. An anthropologist collected eyewitness reports in the early 1920s. Then in 1927, a Russian geologist, Leonid Kulik, led the first scientific expedition to the area. For more than 60 years

**Innokenty Suslov,** a Russian who studied the culture of native groups like the Tungus, photographed Sand Dune Hill in Tunguska in October 1928. Two decades after the mysterious impact, the area was still almost completely devastated. For miles around, trees lay on the ground neatly arrayed, their tops pointing away from the impact site.

after that, the Communist government did not permit foreign scientists to take part in annual expeditions.

Thus the greatest cosmic impact in recorded history remained a near-total scientific mystery for two decades and was treated as almost a state secret for six decades more. In these days of nearly instantaneous worldwide communication, it is hard to imagine that such an event could happen and not be studied immediately by scientists from around the world.

Yet there are still places in the world where few people live and where travel is nearly impossible. Even today, Tunguska is a remote, forbidding wilderness, its land permanently frozen and its hardy, scattered people struggling to survive. Though every summer now brings a new scientific expedition, we still do not know exactly what happened that June morning in 1908.

No part of the "Tunguska object" has been found. Scientists now believe that it weighed about 100 million kilograms (100,000 tons), about 1,700 times as much as the train-car-size nickel-iron meteorite that carved out Meteor Crater. It plowed into the atmosphere until it could no longer withstand the increasing pressure. At about 10 kilometers (6 miles) above the forest, cruising altitude for a passenger airplane, it blew apart.

It may have been a stony asteroid, held together loosely by its weak gravity, but many scientists believe it was a comet. No one knows if its approach caused the unusual white nights before its impact; that could have been a coincidence. It clearly was responsible for the spectacular European and Asian skies of June 30 and the early days of July 1908.

Then its dusty remains settled to Earth, and the Tunguska event became just another scientific curiosity for much of the world. The Tungus people may have been the only ones to "get it right" from the beginning. It was a warning—if not from Ogdy, then from nature. Had that object exploded a few hours later, it would have destroyed the great Russian city of St. Petersburg and killed an estimated 500,000 of the millions of people who lived near there. A few hours earlier, the much smaller city of Anchorage, in the future U.S. state of Alaska, was in the target zone. Its warning to all humanity was this: Cosmic impacts on Earth do not threaten only helpless dinosaurs or reindeer. They also threaten people in every part of the world—people who may be able to turn disaster away, if only they can see the space rock coming in time.

# The Minor Planet Center of the International Astronomical Union displays

up-to-date diagrams on its Web site showing the orbit and position of the major planets, and

the position of the minor planets, both asteroids and comets. As this diagram shows, we have

lots of potentially unwelcome company in our neighborhood of the solar system.

# Will We See It Coming?

WHEN CAROLYN SHOEMAKER joined that "little program" her husband Gene had started, she never expected to become famous. When she saw the squashed comet that became known as Shoemaker-Levy 9, she probably expected no more than a few newspaper articles to mention it. Even when other scientists computed the orbit of Shoemaker-Levy 9 and predicted its collision with Jupiter, she expected the comet and the planet to be the stars of the show.

Carolyn Shoemaker was wrong about that. While the telescopic cameras focused on Jupiter, the network television cameras focused on her, Gene, and their friend David Levy. Suddenly, the three modest comet hunters found themselves cast in the unlikely role of celebrities. Carolyn Shoemaker enthusiastically told the worldwide audience about the experience of comet hunting and the joys of doing science. Levy, a noted science writer, explained the scientific details with his usual clarity.

**To capture** enough light for a telescopic picture of a region of the sky, astronomers need time-exposure photographs. The closer a space object is to Earth, the more rapidly it moves across the telescope's field of view, showing up as a streak in the photograph. Project Spacewatch scientists call such streaks VFMOs, for very fast moving objects. A VFMO often turns out to be an artificial satellite, but sometimes, as in this image of Asteroid 1994 $XM_1$, it turns out to be a newly discovered space rock with an orbit that brings it close enough to Earth to require our attention.

Gene Shoemaker's task was the hardest. He reminded the world that the collisions they were watching across millions of miles of space could happen here. In fact, it has happened here; and if we wait long enough, it will surely happen again. The purpose of the Spacewatch program was to find space rocks on a collision course with Earth. How much warning of a collision will Spacewatch and other asteroid searches give us? Will we be able to do something about it?

The amount of warning will vary from one asteroid and comet to the next. A lot depends on the route it takes to get here. To understand that, let's start by looking more closely at some laws of nature and the path of Comet Shoemaker-Levy 9. To predict a comet's or asteroid's orbit, scientists use the mathematical laws that describe the force of gravity and the way it influences a body's motion. Gravitational forces between two bodies depend on the mass (the amount of matter they contain) of each body and the separation between them.

If you double the mass of either body, you double the force between them. Three times the mass of either one means three times the force, and so on. On Earth, mass is often measured by weighing an object. Weight is the downward force on that object from Earth's gravity. Although most scales actually measure the force of gravity on the object, their markings may indicate the mass instead.

If you double the separation between the bodies, the force drops to one fourth (half of a half) as much. If you triple the distance between them, the force drops to one ninth (a third of a third) as much. Thus a nearby planet can have a much greater gravitational influence on a passing asteroid or comet than the much larger but more distant Sun.

When a small body is in orbit around a large one, the laws of motion and gravity predict that the small body will trace and retrace the same oval path around the large one. Mathematicians call the shape of that path an ellipse, with the large body occupying a certain off-center point called a focus. (An ellipse has two focus points, or foci, each an equal distance from the center. If you shrink the off-center distance to zero, you get a circle.)

For eons, Comet Shoemaker-Levy 9 followed a long elliptical path around the Sun. Because the gravity of the planets also pulled on the comet, its orbit changed a little bit on every loop. In 1929 it passed by Jupiter so closely and at an orbital speed so nearly matching Jupiter's that the giant planet's powerful gravity captured it from the Sun. From that time forward, it followed a long elliptical orbit around its new parent every two years or so.

It often passed close enough to one or another of Jupiter's many moons to feel their gravitational tugs. Each of those encounters changed the shape of the comet's elliptical path a little bit. By the time it had completed about 30 orbits, it was swooping very close to the clouds at the top of Jupiter's atmosphere. When Jupiter's gravity pulled it apart on July 7, 1992, it became a string of pearls on a collision course with history.

According to many planetary scientists, the capture of Comet Shoemaker-Levy 9 demonstrates how important Jupiter is to life on our planet. Its large mass often draws comets toward its orbit, protecting the inner planets from comet strikes. Without Jupiter, those scientists say, life on Earth would have been set back by comet and asteroid strikes many times. It probably would never have evolved past primitive bacteria.

Still, Jupiter may go from hero to villain in our future. Sometimes, instead of capturing a passing comet, it just changes the comet's orbit. Though the chances are very small, that new orbit might send the comet dangerously close to Earth. That unlikely event is one of the worst we could imagine. Our telescopic photographs might first reveal the comet when it is as far away as Saturn. After a few days, we would be able to calculate its orbit well enough to predict that it would pass close to Jupiter.

At that point, calculations of its orbit after passing Jupiter would be very uncertain. A slight difference in its point of closest approach to the giant planet would make a large difference in its later path toward the inner planets. We would watch the comet's path as it passed by Jupiter, and the news could get worse with each day. Unlike the good news that came as we recalculated the orbit of Asteroid 1997 $XF_{11}$, we might not be so lucky. In the worst case, we would find with increasing certainty that the comet was heading right for us. Doomsday might be about a year away before we saw it coming.

The same thing might also happen without the help of Jupiter. A comet that people have never seen before might be

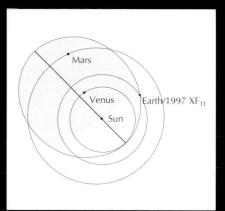

**The orbits of Venus, Earth, Mars, and Asteroid 1997 $XF_{11}$, showing the calculated positions of the planets and the asteroid at the point of its closest approach to Earth in 2028.**

heading our way. That comet would give a little more notice—perhaps two years if we spotted it as far out as Saturn's orbit—but probably not long enough to make a difference.

Fortunately in most cases, we will have much more warning than that. The most likely culprit is not a so-called long-period comet from beyond Jupiter but an asteroid or a short-period comet that orbits closer to the Sun. Most asteroids in the solar system follow harmless paths around the Sun between the orbits of Mars and Jupiter. Some, however, come closer to Earth than that. Those are the "near Earth objects" (NEOs) that scientists worry most about. Year by year, we are finding more and more of them.

Scientists place most known near Earth objects in three classes: Amor asteroids, which cross the orbit of Mars and could come within about 40 million kilometers (about 25 million miles) of Earth; Apollo asteroids, which cross Earth's orbit but are usually farther from the Sun than Earth; and Aten asteroids, which cross Earth's orbit but are usually closer to the Sun. Since the Amors don't cross Earth's orbit, you might wonder why scientists bother looking for them so hard. The problem is that their orbits might shift dangerously. They could collide with another asteroid, or they might come close enough to Earth or Mars to alter their path around the Sun.

Though a cosmic collision between Earth and an Amor, Apollo, or Aten asteroid would be dangerous, we are probably now able to predict it decades in advance. The warning about Asteroid 1997

$XF_{11}$ came 31 years before 2028. If that asteroid were heading for a collision instead of a near miss, people would already be building doomsday shelters and governments would be planning space missions to study, divert, or destroy the deadly rock. With 30 years to study and plan, our chances of success would be quite good.

Despite our many observations, a near miss can sometimes catch us by surprise. It is especially hard to find the Atens, since much of the time they are in a direction too close to the Sun to be seen on Earth. Another reason for a near-miss surprise is the size of the object. We can be confident of spotting a K-T type space rock many years before impact, unless it is a long-period comet never seen before. The same is probably true for most space rocks as large as the Tunguska object; but some NEOs are large enough to cause another Meteor Crater yet small enough to be missed.

The smaller the size, the more space rocks there are and the harder they are to find. We need to keep searching and tracking because we know that the next Meteor Crater or Tunguska impact could take place in a major city, killing hundreds of thousands—even millions—of people. For any major cosmic impact, we want to make sure we have as much warning as possible. With Spacewatch and other programs like it, our chances of getting that warning are improving every year. Still, a warning is only valuable when people are prepared to act on it. We need to find ways to be certain that Ogdy doesn't have the last laugh!

# Saving the Planet

**ONE DAY** in the near or distant future—we can't predict when—scientists in a program like Spacewatch will discover a large space rock on a collision course with Earth. What, if anything, will people or governments be able to do about it?

Let's start with the smallest impact in this book and work toward the largest. Though Meteor Crater formed 50,000 years ago, it is very likely that other rocks the size of the one that caused the crater—about as large and heavy as a train car—have hit Earth since. They may have fallen into the ocean and disappeared from view. Or they may have skipped off the atmosphere. If they came in deeper and exploded in the upper atmosphere, as the Tunguska object did, their damage would have all but vanished within a hundred years.

**If we are faced** with the impact of an asteroid as large as the one that killed the dinosaurs, our only hope will lie in devices at least as powerful as our present nuclear explosives. Will we find a way to keep such devices ready to use on short notice, yet to store them safely for thousands of years or perhaps indefinitely?

The space rock that caused Meteor Crater left its mark because it was mainly nickel-iron. Had it been a more common stony meteorite, it probably would have fallen apart before it could make a hole large and dramatic enough to attract attention after thousands of years. Had it been a very small comet made largely of ice, it would have left only the slightest trace on the ground—a mini Tunguska.

Does that mean we shouldn't worry about space rocks of that size? Hardly! The smaller the object, the more common it is among the cosmic debris. But a large chunk of nickel-iron heading for a city could kill tens or hundreds of thousands of people and cause great destruction. If we spot a space rock large enough to be a Meteor Crater in the making, we will want to act.

What should we do? The first task will be to find out what the rock is made of. Scientists can usually do a chemical analysis by careful measurement of the spectrum—the mix of colors in the sunlight—that reflects from the rock. If it is the kind of object that will likely fall apart in the atmosphere without causing much harm, we will probably keep track of it but do little else. As it nears Earth, scientists will be able to predict its likely point of impact. People unlucky enough to be living in its path might be warned to leave the area for a short time. Meteorites have fallen through roofs of cars and homes, and this one may send a shower of small rocks that will do the same.

However, if it is a nickel-iron or stony-iron rock, the major world governments would probably try to change its course or destroy it. Changing its course is better, and it may be easier if we have enough warning. Like Asteroid 1997 $XF_{11}$, we may spot an object that will make 20 or more orbits before its close encounter. Causing a very slight change in its speed or direction soon after the discovery will be enough to turn an impact or near miss into a passage at a comfortable distance.

We could build a space robot that would land on the rock and attach a small rocket engine to it. Then, when the time and the direction of the rocket engine are right, we would turn it on full blast. A slow, controlled, steady push against a Meteor-Crater-size rock about 100,000 kilograms (220,000 pounds) in mass would easily change its speed by several centimeters (inches) per second. If you can't imagine

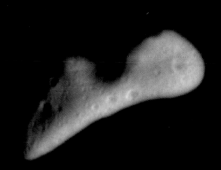

**If we need** to turn away asteroids on collision courses in the future, we need to learn more about them, including what they are made of. In February 2000, the NEAR Shoemaker spacecraft of the Near Earth Asteroid Rendezvous project went into orbit around Eros, a rock about the size and shape of Manhattan Island. Early analysis indicates that it is one of the most primitive objects in the solar system. Its cratered surface shows that it, like all other objects in this part of the solar system, has been involved in cosmic collisions with chunks of matter smaller than itself.

that, think of what large rocket engines can do when launching the space shuttle. Five centimeters (about 2 inches) per second translates to about 1,600 kilometers (about 1,000 miles) per year. In 20 years, that is a distance equal to five times the radius of Earth.

But suppose we don't have enough warning to change its course. Then the robot might carry high explosives like the kind used in construction or mining on Earth. We would hope to break apart the rock, knowing that smaller pieces, even if they hit Earth, would do less damage. We would probably have to send another robot to study the rock first, probing for weak spots where the explosives would do the most good.

What if we spot an object a thousand times more massive, another Tunguska in the making? For that, we would probably need some planning. We could have a few huge rocket engines, like those that launched the Apollo missions to the Moon, ready to be fueled and carried to the deadly rock. They wouldn't change its speed or direction much, but a small change could be a city-saver.

Blowing apart such a rock would require nuclear explosives, but that might be necessary if our warning period is short. The use of nuclear devices creates serious problems, not for scientists but for governments. The major nations of the world have signed treaties to reduce the number of nuclear weapons and to not test them. They have also signed treaties to keep outer space free of nuclear weapons. Their governments have decided that human beings can't be trusted with such terrible power. So we may not have the explosive power when we need it to protect us from a Tunguska rock heading our way.

History tells us that today's national governments are probably right to reduce nuclear explosives. Nations with powerful weapons usually use them against their historical enemies. Even worse, no nation in history has ever lasted much more than a thousand years, and governments are not always wise and just. To prevent misuse of nuclear power, we may have to risk another Tunguska event in a major city.

The situation will be far more serious when the next K-T rock heads our way. If we don't stop it, the cosmic collision will destroy more than a city. It will certainly destroy our environment and civilization, and it may wipe out human life altogether. To change its orbit and protect our world from such a calamity, our only hope may lie in devices as powerful as the nuclear explosives we are still struggling to control.

Because a K-T impact is such a rare event, happening once in tens of millions of years, perhaps we can simply ignore it. The dinosaurs were lucky enough to last 165 million years, but we are smart enough to last longer. In Earth's 4.5 billion years, we humans are the only creatures that ever arose with enough intelligence to save the planet from collisions with giant rocks and snowballs from space. Unlike any living beings before us, we can rewrite the story of cosmic impacts and life on Earth. Our first task will be learning better ways to live with each other. With good fortune, we'll have a few million years to figure out how to do that.

# Author's Note

Writing this book was great fun for me, because I had a chance to learn more about many of my favorite science stories. Of course, not all those stories had a happy ending, especially for the dinosaurs or the Tungus people and their reindeer.

My learning isn't over. I'll continue to read about these stories in books, in magazines and newspapers, and on the World Wide Web. Because I want to share that new learning with you, my personal Web site, www.fredbortz.com, will include updates on these stories plus pointers to other Web sites where you can learn more.

I want to end with special thanks to several of the scientists mentioned in this book. I never met Walter Alvarez, although I attended a memorable lecture where his late father, Luis Alvarez, spoke about his pyramid project. Many years later, Walter was kind enough to respond to my letter requesting an interview for my book *To the Young Scientist* (Franklin Watts, 1997). He suggested that if I really wanted to know about the latest scientific details about the Cretaceous catastrophe, I should interview Frank Asaro instead.

I'm glad I followed his advice. Frank Asaro made certain that I included Helen Michel in the interview, which made it even more memorable and useful. Both of them, though serious about their science, made me smile. They each had a quiet sense of humor that only another scientist could appreciate fully.

As my dedication indicates, Eugene and Carolyn Shoemaker were particularly gracious to me when I interviewed them for *To the Young Scientist.* Carolyn even showed me the films in which she first discovered her "squashed comet."

I regret that Gene did not live to see this book. He died in an automobile accident in the Australian Outback on July 18, 1997, where he and Carolyn had gone to study a likely impact site. His ashes have been scattered in three cosmic impact sites: in Meteor Crater, at a favorite spot in Australia, and in a crater near the Moon's South Pole, carried there by the Lunar Prospector spacecraft. His biggest disappointment in life was being disqualified for a trip to the Moon by a minor health problem. Having a small canister of his ashes on Lunar Prospector added an exclamation point to a life well lived.

While orbiting the Moon, Lunar Prospector detected strong evidence of ice, probably from ancient comet crashes, in the permanently shadowed bottoms of some craters, including the one where it was deliberately crashed as it was running out of fuel. Unfortunately, that impact did not stir up the last piece of evidence the mission scientists were hoping for. That would not have discouraged Gene. Someday, he would have said quietly but firmly, we'll just have to go back to explore that crater some more.

When that someday comes, perhaps you will be the one doing the exploring!

—F. B.

# For Further Information

## BOOKS

Alvarez, Walter. *T. Rex and the Crater of Doom*. Princetown, NJ: Princeton University Press, 1997 (paperback by Vintage Books, 1998).

Bortz, Fred. *To the Young Scientist: Reflections on Doing and Living Science*. Danbury, CT: Franklin Watts, 1997.

Gallant, Roy A. *The Day the Sky Split Apart: Investigating a Cosmic Mystery*. New York: Atheneum Books for Young Readers, 1995.

Levy, David. *Impact Jupiter: The Crash of Comet Shoemaker-Levy 9*. New York: Plenum Press, 1995.

Levy, David. *Comets: Creators and Destroyers*. New York: Touchstone, 1998.

## BOOKS FOR OLDER READERS

Barnes-Svarney, Patricia. *Asteroid: Earth Destroyer or New Frontier*. New York: Plenum Press, 1996.

Dauber, Philip M., and Richard A. Muller. *The Three Big Bangs: Comet Crashes, Exploding Stars, and the Creation of the Universe*. Reading, MA: Addison Wesley, 1996.

Grinspoon, David Harry. *Venus Revealed: A New Look Below the Clouds of Our Mysterious Twin Planet*. Reading, MA: Helix Books, Addison-Wesley Publishing Co., 1997.

Levy, David. *Shoemaker by Levy: The Man Who Made an Impact*. Princeton, NJ: Princeton University Press, 2000.

Lewis, John M. *Rain of Iron and Ice: The Very Real Threat of Comet and Asteroid Bombardment*. Reading, MA: Helix Books, Addison-Wesley Publishing Co., 1996.

McSween, Harry Y., Jr. *Fanfare for Earth: The Origin of Our Planet and Life.* New York: St. Martin's Press, 1997.

Muller, Richard A. Nemesis, *The Death Star: The Story of a Scientific Revolution.* North Pomfret, VT: Weidenfeld and Nicolson, 1988 (Introduction by Luis Alvarez).

Spencer, John R., and Jacqueline Mitton, eds. *The Great Comet Crash: The Collision of Comet Shoemaker-Levy 9 and Jupiter.* New York: Cambridge University Press, 1995 (Foreword and one chapter by Eugene and Carolyn Shoemaker, and marvelous pictures).

## INTERNET RESOURCES

Because the uniform resource locators (URLs) and information on Web sites change rapidly, the information below may be out of date. If the URLs below don't work, go to the author's Web site, "Dr. Fred's Place" (**http://www.fred-bortz.com**). Follow the "hot-links" to "Books by Dr. Fred" and then to "Collision Course." There you will find not only the latest links, but also updated news about cosmic collisions.

NASA asteroid and comet impact pages: **http://impact.arc.nasa.gov**

The Planetary Society's Near Earth Objects Page: **http://neo.planetary.org**

Barringer Meteorite Crater homepage, including great history, science summary, and links: **http://www.barringercrater.com**

Tunguska event information from Roy A. Gallant, Director of the Southworth Planetarium and author of *The Day the Sky Split Apart*: **http://www.usm.maine.edu/~planet/tung.html**

SEDS (Students for the Exploration and Development of Space) Comet Shoemaker-Levy 9 homepage: **http://seds.lpl.arizona.edu/sl9/sl9.html**

NASA Jet Propulsion Laboratory Comet Shoemaker-Levy 9 homepage: **http://www.jpl.nasa.gov/sl9**

National Space Science Data Center Comet Shoemaker-Levy 9 homepage: **http://nssdc.gsfc.nasa.gov/planetary/comet.html**

NASA Lunar Prospector homepage: **http://lunar.arc.nasa.gov**

# Index

Page numbers in *italics* refer to illustrations.

Acid rain, 32

Alvarez, Luis, 27–30, *31*, 65

Alvarez, Walter, 22–25, 27–29, *31*, 65

Amor asteroids, 56

Anchorage, Alaska, 49

Apennine Mountains, 24

Apollo asteroids, 56

Apollo moon missions, 62

*Armageddon* (movie), 5

Asaro, Frank, 23, 29–30, *31*, 65–66

Asteroid 1994 XM$_1$, *52*

Asteroid 1997 XF$_{11}$, 5–7, 50, *55*, 55–57, 61

Aten asteroids, 56, 57

Barringer, Daniel, 16–17

Barringer Meteorite Crater (*see* Meteor Crater, Arizona)

Callisto, 43

Cambrian Period, 27

Carbon dioxide, 32

Catastrophism, 23, 24, 34

Cenozoic Era, 25, 26

Chao, Edward, 18

Chicxulub crater, 34, *35*, 43

Clay layer, 24–25, *25*, *26*, 27, 29

Clementine mission, 20

Climate, 22

Coesite, 18, *19*, 33

Comet Shoemaker-Levy 9, 6, 7, *36–37*, 38–43, *42*, 51, 52, 54

Continents, 22

Cretaceous Period, 6, 25–27, 32, 41

Darwin, Charles, 23

Davy crater, 43

*Deep Impact* (movie), 5

Dinosaurs, extinction of, 21, 25, 26, 32

Earthquakes, 18, 46
Ellipse, 53
Eros, *61*
Evolution, 23

Focus, 53
*Foraminifera* (forams), 24, *25*
Fossils, 24, 25

Galileo spacecraft, 41
Gallant, Roy A., 66
Ganymede, 43
Global warming, 31, 32
Gravity, 53

Hardy, David, *15*, 15
Hubble Space Telescope, 9, 41

International Astronomical Union dia-
    gram, *50*
Internet resources, 69
Iridium, 6, 21, 27–29

Jupiter, 6, 21, 38, 40, 41, 43, 51,
    54–56
Jurassic Period, 26

Khefren pyramid, 27
K-T boundary, 27, 33, 34, 57, 63
Kulik, Leonid, 46

Levy, David, 38, *39*, 51
Limestone, 24, *25*, *26*, 27
Lunar Prospector spacecraft, 20, 66

Madsen, Beth, 18
Mars, 21, *55*, 56
Mercury, 21
Mesozoic Era, 21, 24–26
Meteor Crater, Arizona, 16–18, 33, 48,
    57, 58, 60
Michel, Helen, 23, 29–30, *31*,
    66
Milky Way galaxy, 9
Moon, 12–13, 43, 66–67
    craters of, 19–21, *20*
Mount Wilson, California, 46

National Aeronautics and Space
    Administration (NASA), 21
Near Earth Asteroid Rendezvous proj-
    ect, 61
Near Earth objects (NEOs), 56
NEAR Shoemaker spacecraft, 61
Neptune, 21
Neutron activation analysis, 29
Nickel-iron, 60, 61
Nitric acid, 32
Noctilucent clouds, 45
Nuclear fusion, 10
Nuclear weapons, 62–63

Ogdy (god), 46, 49, 57

Pike's Peak, 43
Planetesimals, 10, 28
Planets, 10, 16, 21. (*see also* specific
  planets)
Plate tectonics, 23, 33
Podkamennaya (Stony) Tunguska River,
  46

Quartz, 18, 33

Rocky Mountains, 33

St. Petersburg, 49
Saturn, 21, 55, 56
*Scaglia rossa*, 24, 25, 27, 29
*Science* magazine, 30
Scotti, James V., *11*
Seasons, 12
Seismographs, 46
Shoemaker, Carolyn, 34, 37–40, *39*,
  51, 66
Shoemaker, Eugene ("Gene"), 16,
  18–21, 33, 34, 37–39, *39*, 51–52,
  66, 67
Siberia, 6, 7, 43, 44–46, *47*, 48–49,
  57, 58

Solar nebula, *8*, 9–10
Solar system, 9
Spaceguard UK, 15
Spacewatch program, 52, 57, 58
Spectrum, 60
Stereomicroscopy, 37
Sun, 10, 12, 53, 54, 56
Supernova, 9

Tertiary Period, 26–27
Tides, 12
Triassic Period, 26
Tsunami, 33, 34
Tunguska event of 1908, 6, 7, 43,
  44–46, *47*, 48–49, 57, 58

Uniformitarianism, 23, 24, 34
University of California, 21
Uranus, 21

Venus, 21, *55*
VFMOs (very fast moving objects),
  52
Volcanoes, 18

White nights, 45, 48

Yucatan Peninsula, 34